For Real?

unicorns

Dana Meachen Rau

Cavendish Square

To the Tuesday Morning Writers, who all have wonderful stories to tell
—D.M.R.

With thanks to Mark A. Norell, Chairman and Curator-in-Charge, Fossil Reptiles, Amphibians, and Birds, American Museum of Natural History, New York, for the careful review of this manuscript

Published by by Cavendish Square Publishing

Cavendish Square Publishing, LLC
2544 Clinton Street, Buffalo, NY 14224

Website: cavendishsq.com

Editor: Christina Gardeski
Publisher: Michelle Bisson
Art Director: Anahid Hamparian
Series Designer: Virginia Pope

1 3 5 6 4 2

Library of Congress Cataloging-in-Publication Data
Rau, Dana Meachen, 1971-
Unicorns / by Dana Meachen Rau.
p. cm. — (Bookworms chapter books: for real?)
Includes bibliographical references and index.
Summary: "Explores the real story behind unicorns, why myths and legends grew around them, and how to sort between fact and fiction" —Provided by publisher.
ISBN 978-0-7614-4864-8
1. Unicorns—Juvenile literature. I. Title.
GR830.U6R38 2011
398.24'54--dc22
2009052357

Cover illustration by Vincent Nguyen

Photo Research by Bill Smith Group
The photographs in this book are used by permission and through the courtesy of: 1 (all) © Buddy Mays/Alamy; 3 (bl) Keren Su/China Span/Getty Images; 4 (bkgd) © Hugh Threlfall / Alamy; 6 (l) © Taily, 2009. Used under license from Shutterstock.com; 7 (t) © Ashley Cooper/Alamy; 8 (bkgd) Keren Su/China Span/Getty Images; 10 (t) Erich Lessing/Art Resource, NY; 11 (tr) French School/The Bridgeman Art Library/Getty Images; 13 (bkgd) © Francis G. Mayer/Corbis; 14 (bkgd) Alinari/Art Resource, NY; 16 (t) Finsiel/Alinari/Art Resource, NY; 18 (bkgd) Ben Cranke/The Image Bank/Getty Images; 21 (t) Paul Nicklen/National Geographic/Getty Images.

unicorns

Chapter 1

Unicorns have been the subject of stories and art for thousands of years.

Not an Ordinary Horse

Imagine walking in the woods. You spot a horse by a river bending to take a drink. When you look closer, you see this animal is larger than an **ordinary** horse. It is pure white, with one long horn in the center of its forehead. Can it be a unicorn?

Through history, people have told many stories about unicorns. In some stories, these animals are gentle, pure, and loving. In other tales, unicorns are **fierce**, strong, and fast. They like to be alone and are impossible to catch.

People believed unicorns were real. Reports of these creatures came from India, Africa, and Asia. Stories came from Scandinavia [skan-duh-NEY-vee-uh] and even the United States.

Many tales from history are filled with weird creatures. A hippogriff was part horse and part eagle. A sphinx [SFINKS]

Some stories told of gentle, tame unicorns, while others described them as fierce, wild creatures.

The lion and unicorn make up the coat of arms of Britain, one of their national symbols.

had a lion's body and a human head. Unicorns, however, were not as strange. A unicorn looked like a horse, but with a lion's tail, a beard like a billy goat, and one long horn. That was not so hard to believe. Many folks believed in unicorns, even if they had never seen one.

Chapter 2

Not all unicorns looked like horses. The qilin looked more like a dragon and brought good luck.

Unicorns in History

Unicorn **myths** may have started almost 5,000 years ago. The Chinese tell of the *qilin* [CHEE-lin]. A qilin was a mix of a deer and a dragon with one horn. The gentle qilin had a beautiful voice. It would not hurt other living things, and could walk on grass without crushing the blades. This animal visited great leaders in China and brought them good luck.

The *karkadann* [kar-ka-DANN] was a unicorn from Persian stories. Persia (now called Iran) was an area found in the Middle East. The karkadann looked like a hippopotamus, and was not gentle like the qilin. The karkadann was a dangerous warrior. It battled other animals with its sharp horn on deserts and grasslands.

Around 2,400 years ago, a Greek doctor named Ctesias [TEE-she-us] wrote about unicorns. He described a one-horned animal living in India. Many other Greeks and Romans wrote about Ctesias's unicorns, too. News spread about these special animals.

Early Bibles also mention unicorns. In the third century, the Bible was rewritten in the Greek language. This holy book told of a strong, large animal with a horn. So the **translators** used the Greek word *monoceros*, which means one horn. Later, the word became *unicornis*. Many believed in unicorns because they were written about in these early Bibles.

Belief in unicorns was most popular in the Middle Ages—the time of castles, kings, and knights. Scientists at the time wrote about unicorns in their big books of animals. Artists wove pictures of unicorns into their **tapestries**. Hunters told stories about unicorns they saw in the woods, and the wild folks they spotted riding on their backs.

In this painting, unicorns are included among the many animals in Noah's ark.

Long ago, scientists drew pictures of the animals they had seen or heard of. Unicorns were included in their books.

Unicorn tales lasted for a long time. In the early 1800s, however, a scientist who studied animal skulls claimed unicorns could not be real. He said a one-horned creature like a unicorn could not exist because of the way bones grow in similar animals. Soon, fewer people believed in unicorns. Today, most people think unicorns are just animals in stories.

Artists wove unicorn stories into their tapestries. This one shows a captured unicorn at the end of a hunt.

Chapter 3

Hunters tried to catch unicorns. But only young girls had the power to tame them.

Magical Horns

Stories told that a unicorn's horn had special powers. The animal would dip its horn in a river. Then the water would be clean for other animals to drink.

People thought the horn was powerful against **poison**. So they wanted to own these horns. But how could they catch a unicorn? Some tales described unicorns as quick, strong, and dangerous to fight. They used their horns like swords. Hunters had to think of ways to trick unicorns to catch them.

According to myths, only a young girl could catch a unicorn. Hunters in these stories brought young girls on the hunt. The girl would sit in a clearing in the woods. The unicorn would come out to see her. It would become gentle and **tame**. Then the hunter could catch it.

Rich people made all sorts of horns into drinking cups. This one is made from a buffalo horn.

In the Middle Ages, **merchants** bought and sold animal horns. Horns sold as "unicorn" horns cost a lot. The rich made them into drinking cups. They used them to check for poison in their food. **Apothecaries** used ground up "unicorn" horn to make medicines. They claimed that medicine with unicorn horn could cure someone who had been poisoned.

According to some myths, if a unicorn dipped its horn in a stream, the water would be pure for all the animals to drink.

Chapter 4

An African antelope called an oryx might be one of the animals people mistook for unicorns.

Unusual Animals

Can unicorns be real? Many stories from history mention unicorns. People used what they thought were unicorn horns for hundreds of years. If unicorns were not real, where did the tales come from? What horns did they use?

A type of **antelope**, called an oryx [AWR-iks], lives in Africa. It has two horns. Maybe travelers saw an oryx from the side or from far away and thought it had one horn instead. Travelers might have seen a rhinoceros. A rhinoceros has a long horn on its nose.

Merchants in the Middle Ages probably thought they were selling real unicorn horns. The horns they sold, however, might have been from **narwhals**. A narwhal is a type of whale that lives in cold arctic waters. It has a single tusk growing out of its upper jaw that is actually a tooth. Sailors and fishermen found these horns on beaches or killed narwhals for their horns. The horn looked like the ones described in unicorn stories.

From early in history, people ground up horns from all kinds of animals. The Chinese used rhinoceros horns. It was common to use this powder in medicines. The drinking cups that royal people used to protect themselves from poison might have been made from narwhal or rhinoceros horns.

Maybe unicorns did live long ago. After all, the world is full of many unusual animals. Some animals that once lived are now **extinct**. Some animals are born different than the rest of their kind. Maybe a goat or antelope was once born with only one horn instead of two. Someone might report that they saw a new one-horned creature.

Travelers shared stories about the many animals they had seen or heard of during their journeys. People heard descriptions of weird creatures, such as elephants with

Narwhals are odd looking sea animals. Their horn is actually one long tooth!

snakelike noses or scaly crocodiles with huge jaws. They seemed even stranger than a horse with one horn.

You have probably seen animals with long necks, curly tails, and rainbow beaks. What's so unusual about a unicorn?

Glossary

antelope [AN-tuh-lohp] an animal with horns that lives in Africa and Asia

apothecaries [uh-POTH-uh-ker-ees] people who made and sold medicine

extinct [ek-STINGKT] no longer living

fierce [FEERS] very mean and dangerous

merchants [MUR-chuhnts] people who buy and sell things

myths [MITHS] stories people tell to explain the past or describe unbelievable creatures

narwhals [NAHR-wahls] whales that live in cold arctic waters and have long tusks

ordinary [AWRD-ner-ee] plain or usual

poison [POI-zuhn] something that can hurt or kill someone if they drink or eat it

tame [TAYM] not wild

tapestries [TAP-uhs-trees] heavy cloths with pictures woven into them

translators [trans-LAYT-uhrs] people who rewrite something from one language to another

Books to Discover

Di Francesco, Mia. *Unicorns: Magical Creatures from Myth and Fiction*. New York: Tangerine Press/Scholastic, 2007.

Penner, Lucille Recht. *Unicorns*. New York: Random House Books for Young Readers, 2005.

Weigelt, Udo. *The Legendary Unicorn*. New York: North-South Books, 2004.

Yolen, Jane. *Where Have the Unicorns Gone?* New York: Simon & Schuster Children's Publishing, 2003.

WEBSites TO Explore

All About Unicorns

www.allaboutunicorns.com/

Mythic Creature Exhibit:

The American Museum of Natural History

www.amnh.org/exhibitions/mythiccreatures

National Geographic: Narwhal

http://animals.nationalgeographic.com/animals/mammals/narwhal.html

The Unicorn Tapestries

www.metmuseum.org/explore/Unicorn/hunt_unicorn_transcript.htm

Index

About the Author

Dana Meachen Rau is the author of more than 250 books for children. She has written about many nonfiction topics from her home office in Burlington, Connecticut. Mrs. Rau has never seen a unicorn, but she did ride a mule to the bottom of Bryce Canyon in Utah.

With thanks to the Reading Consultants:

Nanci R. Vargus, Ed.D., is an assistant professor of elementary education at the University of Indianapolis.

Beth Walker Gambro is an adjunct professor at the University of Saint Francis in Joliet, Illinois.